The Month of the Asparagus

Keith Armstrong

Ward Wood Publishing
www.wardwoodpublishing.co.uk

Published by Ward Wood Publishing
6 The Drive
Golders Green
London NW11 9SR
www.wardwoodpublishing.co.uk

The right of Keith Armstrong to be identified as author of this work has been asserted by him in accordance with the Copyright, Designs and Patent Act, 1988.
Copyright © 2011 Keith Armstrong
ISBN: 978-0-9566602-9-9
British Library Cataloguing in Publication Data. A CIP record for this book can be obtained from the British Library.

All rights reserved. No part of this publication may be reproduced, stored in a retrieval system, or transmitted in any form or by any means, electronic, mechanical, photocopying, recording or otherwise without either the prior written permission of the publishers. This book may not be lent, hired out, resold or otherwise disposed of by way of trade in any form of binding or cover other than that in which it is published, without the prior consent of the publishers.

Designed and typeset in Palatino Linotype
by Ward Wood Publishing.
Cover design by Mike Fortune-Wood
Cover panel photos: Common Public License,
taken from several versions of *The Tacuinum Sanitatis*,
15th century Lombardy translations of *Taqwim al-sihha*,
an 11th century Islamic book of health and well being.

Printed and bound in Great Britain by
Imprint Digital, Seychelles Farm,
Upton Pyne, Exeter EX5 5HY, UK

For my mother and sister

Contents

At Anchor	9
Marsden Rock	10
For 'Cuny'	12
Maud Watson, Florist	15
Fat Man Lodged on Dog Leap Stairs	16
Two Poems for Thomas Bewick,	
Celebrated Engraver on Wood	
Amen Corner	18
Return to Cherryburn	19
Man of Music in Paxton	20
Tales of Spittal	22
Call Laurence Stephen Lowry!	24
Girl in a Spittal Window	26
Alnwickdote	27
Three Saint Cuthbert Poems	
Don't Trust Saints	28
Prophets	29
This Burning Beam	30
Greylag Geese	32
Elvet Bridge	33
The Golden Room	34
Grand Hotel	36
For David Stephenson	38
Rooks at Bunratty Castle	39
Constance	40
Flying Into Tübingen Airspace	42
Tübingen Webcam	44
Dawn Chorus, Corrensstrasse 45	46
Hermann Hesse in the Gutter	47
Hier Kotzte Goethe (Goethe Puked Here)	48
The Month of the Asparagus	50
Lange Gasse 18	51
City Poet	52
Backwater	55

Vismarkt	56
Keep an Eye on the Martini Tower for Me	58
The Lack of Music on a Den Bosch Estate	60
Groningen Horses	62
Swan Song	63
Sky the Guide Dog	64
Poem for a Blues Harmonica	65
Chet – From a Window	66
Love Poem	68
For Paul	69
Grapes in Bulgaria	70
My Lady Dentist	71
So Don't Come to My Funeral	72
Leaving Friends/Friends Leaving	74
We Change at Limerick Junction	76

About the Author

Acknowledgements

The Month of the Asparagus

At Anchor

Birds hurl themselves at the leaping Tyne;
I catch them through the evening window.
It is cold for the time.
My throat is stuffy with poems left unsaid.
Weary troubadour, I am
swimming with visions of ancient European tours.
Now I have landed, with my seagull wings,
in Haydon Bridge to honour a famous son.
I am lodged in the Anchor Hotel,
another lonely night of a whirlwind life:
lorries howl around me
and I can hear a village trembling
in the blinding dark.
Restlessly at anchor,
I cannot sleep for the ghost of John Martin
lighting up my room
with dynamic visions
and the thunderous clatter of his wild dreams.
Stuck in the rut of my own poetry
I force myself to sleep,
bobbing by the river
under the fantastic sky.
The community lights shine on my imagination
and the screams of swifts
make a life worthwhile.

John Martin (1789-1854). Historical Painter. Born Haydon Bridge, Northumberland 1789. Died Isle of Man 1854.

Marsden Rock

Sensational Rock
swimming in light.
Bird cries clinging to ancient ledges,
Kittiwakes smashing against time.
What tales you could tell.

Your face is so moody,
flickers with breezes,
crumbles in a hot afternoon.

Climbing your powdery steps
we look down on the sea
thrashing at you.

We join a choir of birds at your peak,
cry out to the sky
in good spirits.

Nesting for the sake of it,
our lyrics are remnants on the shore.

We keep chipping away,
do we not?

We slip
through the pebbles,
splashing
with babies.

We leave our mark,
a grain
on the ancient landscape.

We go.

We dance like the sunlight
on your scarred body:

tripping,
falling,
singing

away.

For 'Cuny'

'Search where Ambition rag'd, with rigour steel'd;
Where Slaughter, like the rapid lightning, ran;
And say, while mem'ry weeps the blood-stain'd field,
Where lies the chief, and where the common man?'
                                                    John Cunningham

'Unto thy dust, sweet Bard! adieu!
Thy hallow'd shrine I slowly leave;
Yet oft, at eve, shall Mem'ry view
The sun-beam ling'ring on thy grave.'
                                                    David Carey

This week an elegant tombstone, executed by Mr Drummond of this town, was set up in St John's churchyard to the memory of the late ingenious Mr John Cunningham. The following is the inscription thereon:

'Here lie the Remains of JOHN CUNNINGHAM.
Of his Excellence as a Pastoral Poet,
His Works will remain a Monument
For Ages
After this temporary Tribute of Esteem
Is in Dust forgotten.
He died in Newcastle, Sept 18, 1773,
Aged 44.'

The ritual slaughter
of traffic
hurling itself
against the furious economy,
the commerce of suffering,
the pain of money,
nudges your bones
in this graveyard of hollow words.
I hear you liked a jar,

well, here's me
sprinkling
your precious monument
with a little local wine,
lubricating the flowers
that burst from your pastoral verses.

You toured the boards like me,
torn like me,
with your heart,
terrific heart,
pouring real blood on your travelling sleeve.
Oh, my God!
Your lips trembled
with a delicate love
for the fleeting joy,
the melancholic haze,
the love in a mist,
that Tom Bewick sketched in you
and Mrs Slack fed
as you passed along
this way and that,
despair in your eyes.
The fact was
you were not born
for the rat race
of letters,
the ducking and fawning
for tasteless prizes,
the empty bloated rivalry,
the thrust of their bearded egos.
You wanted wonder,
the precise touch
of the sun on your grave,
the delicious kiss
that never comes back.
I'm with you, 'Cuny',
in this Newcastle Company of Comedians;

I'm in your clouds of drunken ways;
I twitch with you
in my poetic nervousness
along Westgate Road.
And the girls left their petals for you
like I hope they do for me
in the light of the silver moon,
thinking of your pen
scratching stars into the dark sky.

Maud Watson, Florist

bred in a market arch
a struggle
in a city's armpit

that flower
in your time-rough hands
a beautiful girl in a slum alley

all that kindness in your face

and you're right

the times are not what they were
this England's not what it was

flowers shrink in that crumbling vase
dusk creeps in on a cart

and Maud the sun is choking

Maud this island's sinking

and all that swollen sea is

the silent majority

waving

Fat Man Lodged on Dog Leap Stairs

He pounded the cobbles
of the Castle Garth,
bowling along
with his brain hanging over his neck
and his belly
looming over his huge pants.
His overeducated head
weighed a ton
and bore down
on an arse
fattened on home-made pies.
He was carrying a plan
for the working classes
but forgot his heart was too small,
dwarfed by his huge mouth
and an expensive ego.
He had a board meeting to go to,
the big fart,
and he sweated grants
as he blundered along
to the narrow alley.
He was far too broad of beam really
but he was late for everything,
including his funeral,
and thrust his plates of meat
onto the slippery steps.
History closed in on him,
the Black Gate,
the Keep,
as if to tell him
it wasn't his,
as if to say
'Get out of my town'.
He squeezed himself onto this narrow stairway
and, like his poetry,
got stuck.

He coudn't move
for his lack of lyricism.
The Fat Man
was firmly lodged
on Dog Leap Stairs
and the crows
began to gather
to swoop
and pick
the bloated power
from his face.

Two Poems for Thomas Bewick, Celebrated Engraver on Wood

Amen Corner

The starlings en masse
roost here now.
They blend with the dark trees
in the twilight
by Bewick's shadowy workshop.
Under the cathedral spire
they shriek and gossip
in the chill;
chit-chat of more weather.

Thomas, I think that
you could speak to birds,
knew them as you drew their words
in woodblocks.
You coaxed them from their very eggs,
uncaged them –
let them sing on the page.

Return to Cherryburn

Drawing
clear of the city
you carved your name
in dog barks
and bird cries.
Your infant eyes
kept seeing
the devils in bushes
and the gods
in thrushes.

You loved
to scratch a living.

Avoiding the faces
of strange places
you dreamed of always
being a boy,
a bird or a fish,
awash in the light
of a dark wood:

a cherry burn.

Footprints home

to remember.

Man of Music in Paxton

(For Gary, Jane & Archie)

There's a man in Paxton
who is researching stars
and that musical telescope of his
stares out of the village window
to pierce a broader darkness.

There is a universal symphony in his breath,
picked up from the folk whistling
in the rain-kissed street.
There's a child singing across the borders
and the sky is a chorus
of screaming clouds.

Our man of music in Paxton
scratches notes as he opens his mind.
He calls out
under the leaping rainbow
for a song to enter
his soul.

He wants to name a star after his wife.
He wants to write Jane a song.
There is nothing more beautiful than the sight of Space:
'Nothing more terrible than the beauty of music,' he says.

And while his songs are soaring to the stars,
in the name of his radiant life,
he knows his Dad's bones are cracking with age
and he knows there are days
when his guitar will sob
in the village darkness.

But, tonight, he has named a star 'Jane'
and, while life is forever such struggle,
he has written a lovely song in Paxton
and taught his son Archie to dance in the sky.

Tales of Spittal

This small space
for tall tales,
the leprous tongues of centuries,
hospitalised gossips,
words drifting out of ward windows
on a dripping wet afternoon.
Church reduced to a hung silence,
closed hearts
ready for a drink.

And there's this man
like a tea leaf in the corners
of the Blenheim or the Red Lion or The Albion.
He's gagging for a chat about the old days,
it's on the lips of driftwood
swirling in the blown down days.

Tug the fruit machine,
wallop down a pie-eyed dream.
The ghosts of Victorian ladies
hiss along the promenade
as we are hit in the face
with sepia breezes.
They come from North Sea places
and from Kelso,
Selkirk and Hawick;
they ripple the surface of the sea
and the leaves in the border forests.

Take the ancient waters,
sips of iron and sulphur,
bathe yourself in history and grime.
Pellets of sleet,
hail a watery charabanc drive,
run a hot bath
down the prom prom prom.
And let the keen and callous wind
whip up the skirts of the Tweedside girls
so you can dance for your lives.

We are the Spittal folk,
the old Pierrots,
our songs are shattered
on ancient rocks.
Our children skip through the clutter of news.

Bless them,
bless young hearts.
Splash in Bishop's Water,
in fishing places,
songs of herring and of salmon.

Spittal Rovers
sing again.
Leap for breath
in the ways of spring.

Call Laurence Stephen Lowry!

Shy man
in the Castle Hotel.
He clangs the bell
and leans over Marjorie,
chats her up with a sketch.
She giggles at his shyness.

His old boots squeak the floorboards of memory,
his heart is sad and soaked in loneliness.

Eyes peel in the morning sun
and off he heads
for Spittal light,
on he wanders
pale and drawn over the seaside stubble.

Strides our man Lowry,
bold along the seafront
in search of a hand to hold.

Day damp,
frown on this paintbrush,
town on his palette.

Clouds scud over Spittal,
days are lost.
Smoke from the factory,
dreams from the chimney.

This wee girl in red pops up,
bobs like a buoy on his canvas.
He wants her smile,
she poses one for him.
Grab the moment.

Lowry lost in driftwood,
reeking of fish.
Wander to bed,
dream of the swans
and the mouth of the Tweed.

Girl in a Spittal Window

Glancing moment,
chance look.
I was wondering
where to go,
what to do
in the seaside fret.
I am growing
misty with dreams:
welcome to my Spittal World.
I am little in this universe,
the sun is falling,
the stars are poised.
The window cleaner
will come in the morning
and wipe yesterday
away.

Alnwickdote

These rough stones,
carried for miles to build
such a castle,
mounted on fields
of bitter-sweet slopes.

Stoned lions,
countrified gargoyles
hunch, unpouncing;
their stiff glares fixed
on us fee-paying visitors,
taking a stroll through
the dusty chapters,
the library-dungeons.

And I would suppose
this afternoon to be,
for us, some piece of history,
both strolling through
crisis after crisis,
hearts beating heartbeats
and blood warm, flowing
through us as we walk between
such cold walls,
older than a duke,
but never as wise as this love of mine
nor as fragile as
that historic moment inside the castle
when once you smiled at me
so wonderfully.

Alnwick Castle, Northumberland

Three Saint Cuthbert Poems

Don't Trust Saints

I wouldn't trust Saints,
goody goody two shoe Christians –
they wouldn't pull me out of the mire
with their do-gooding ways.
I do my praying in the trough,
sweaty trotters grubbing together,
not in anyone's heaven
but rooting in the soil
for bread.
Don't get me wrong,
I like a drop of wine
with me nosh,
and I can put the fear of God
in me neighbours
to keep them off me land;
shoot them stone dead if I have to.
They can go to Hell
for all I care,
whole lot of them:
Poets and Peasants,
Pipers and Plovers.
I just get on with growing me crops,
no time for preaching Love and Hate.
This Northumbrian sun is all I know,
and the gannets swooping over me.
What I can't touch or feel or smell or taste
is no good to me:
you can't eat hymns
but I can catch rabbits.

Prophets

The bones of Prophets
rot in this sacred land.
Cuthbert's spirit soars with the gulls
over the ancient ground.
North Country hearts
beat with the songs and ballads
of missing centuries;
lyrics in the rough wind,
notes in the margins.
The Saints and the Scholars
scribble down the years -
but who can make sense of it all?
Bind up the volumes
of human endeavour
in this vast universe,
let the dust of our thoughts
feed the insects.
In truth, Northumberland is
a bleak land
held together by dreams,
fantasies of us all being Saints:
an open slate
still wet with the drizzle
of the scribe's pen.

This Burning Beam

This burning beam
that did for Aidan,
Bamburgh's finest
fallen King of Northumbria,
in ashes.
Palaces of Pretence,
Gefrin on a summer's afternoon,
basking by the Glen
where Paulinus
baptised us with pelting sleet,
and where the late Josephine Butler
spread her kind smile
for the welfare of wor women folk,
for the goodness of touch.

Oh Edwin oh Oswald,
oh Ida oh Hussa,
carry my head in your hands.
My mighty warriors of Christ,
is that you in the curlew's cry?
Is that you in the breeze on my face?

Cuthbert's a hermit crab,
Wonder-worker of England,
and I am an empty shell of a man,
talking to birds
because they make more sense of my life.

Listen to me Bede, I'm the Universal Soldier,
I have rubbed ointment
on Cuthbert's sore knee,
ridden with him across the sheep-snow hills,
and bathed his suppurating ulcer
in red wine.
Light a torch for me
for I am no Saint.
Yet I speak
the Gospel Truth:

Grant to me, Lord Christ,
for this pilgrim journey through life,
Your ready hand to guide me, your light to go before me,
Your protection to guard me from evil,
Your peace to rest within me, your love to sustain me,
That through all the joys and sorrows that meet me
I may know the promise of your abiding strength,
Until I reach my final homecoming with you forever.

Greylag Geese

Spearing dusk,
three thousand and one geese
flap over hills to roost.

Instinctively moved,
urged on by God knows what,
they cling to water.

Behind stone walls we watch.
Witnesses,
silent
in this kind of homage.

The evening is a prayer.
A red hymn,
the sky soars around us.

Air filled with feathers.
Bird talk clatters,
goose-pimples our skin.

Some friend says:
'You're right, we're all of us
living on the brink.'

How mad are we.
How brutalised to have such power
to blow up geese.

Elvet Bridge

(inspired by Guillaume Apollinaire)

Under Elvet Bridge the rain
flows with our loves.
Must I recall again?
Joy always used to follow after pain.

The days pass, the weeks pass
all in vain.
Time spent or misspent,
love won't come back again.

Under Elvet Bridge the rain
flows with our loves.
Must I recall again?
Joy always used to follow after rain.

The Golden Room

'Was it for nothing that the little room,
All golden in the lamplight, thrilled with golden
Laughter from hearts of friends that summer night?'
                                        Wilfrid Gibson

I'm as happy as a daffodil
this day;
sunshine flows around me
over fences,
leaping
with the joy of my poetry.

I am Lord Pretty Field,
a tipsy aristocrat of verse,
become full of myself
and country booze
in the Beauchamp Arms.

Under branches frothy with blossom
I carry a torch from Northumberland
for Wilfrid Gibson
and his old mates;
for Geraldine
I bear
my Cheviot heart
in Gloucester ciderlight.

We can only catch
a petal from the slaughter,
a bloom
to ease the melancholy
of a Dymock dusk;
hear laughter
over the gloomy murmurs
of distant wars.

A swirling rook cries out
across St Mary's spire
in dialect
as I climb
back to my White House room
to dream of an England gone,
and a flash of whisky
with Abercrombie.

For Wilfrid you are still
a singing star,
drenched in balladry;
and this I know:
I will keep your little songs alive
in this Golden Room in my heart
and, in my Hexham's market place,
rant for you
and cover
all our love
with streaming daffodils.

Grand Hotel

When completed in 1867 the Grand Hotel, Scarborough, was one of the largest hotels in the world. The hotel's distinctive yellow brickwork was made locally in Hunmanby. The building is designed around the theme of time: four towers to represent the seasons, 12 floors for the months of the year, 52 chimneys for the weeks, and, originally, 365 bedrooms.

We yellow
in the fretting mist,
in a cold and massive sea
of worn out efforts.
To survive another dying day
we group together
in a futile way
to seek out the haunting touch of warmth.
We have finished
with love,
we have come to die
among the lifts and dumb waiters
of a Grand Hotel no longer grand,
gone back to seed.
We choke on our fish and chips,
our battered skin
crumbling like these faded walls.
We are a calendar
of bent and aching hours,
sick with the germs of an English decay.
We hang about,
waiting for the coach
to take us away
and burn us
and our dreams.
Once we sang
in the midst of springtime hope,
our holiday hymns full of a rash desire.
Now we come here

to die in this recession,
on this grim evening,
thinking of the empire lost
and why we fought for it,
things gone wrong
with our poor children
who have inherited
our tears.

For David Stephenson

David Stephenson was a deep friend –
I met him through books.
He came from Carlisle
with that intense and craggy look.
We studied life together,
smoked Full Strength
and sipped Real Ale.
He liked his women big.
I learnt from him
to visit pubs at lunchtimes,
to end up pissed in lectures
but, most of all,
to read the letters of Van Gogh,
the diaries of Franz Kafka,
to go inside
the jazz
of Ornette Coleman
and Cecil Taylor.
David told me that
'Most people are thick'
and, as a socialist of a kind,
I sometimes think he had a point.
I wonder where he is today.
Back across country I surmise,
smoking and looking at the sunrise
with a fat woman kissing his neck,
listening to Mingus
and the sky.

Rooks at Bunratty Castle

We're Macnamara's crows,
rooting for sticks and twigs in Limerick days.
We peck the flesh from Lord Gort's arse,
from the hangers-on to his rich pickings.
We sweep our turbulent wings across the Shannon,
swimming in the Atlantic winds,
flailing over the airport.
We're building our own
branches of castles,
screaming rebel rants at you below.
Us rooks
have seen the Vikings and the Stoddarts
rave and die.
We are a black brood
swarming though history,
watching you feckless humans
scrap over misery.

See how our wings beat
with the moment's surf.

How dark our hearts grow
with suffering.

Constance

'Hours, more brief than the kiss
Of a beam on the lake that is mourning,
Than the song of a bird on the wing,
Which drops down like pearls from above'
                    Annette von Droste-Hülshoff (1797-1848)

I have lakes for eyes today
on a ferry across memory.
I am reaching for friends,
skirting boundaries.
My arms thrash in wild waves.
In this moody vista
of wild dreams
and legends,
the horseman rides
his panting steed
across the ice of cold lake kisses,
not knowing, in all this darkness,
just how close he is
to a plunging death.
The swirling weeds
that wrap themselves
around our shaking bodies
are full of drowned days
and gulped-down sunshine.

Look! These Alps are clouds today
and the mountains pile up in the sky.
The line is thin between
fantastic vision
and suicide.
Another sip and I'll slash my wrists,
gash the sky with blood,
dash poems on a promenade
awash with tourist trash
and the curse of cash.

Knowing looks
she gives me,
this mighty Constance.
She gleams with sunlight
and sadness,
her red wave hits the mountain's edge.
I want to get to know her more,
to sail in her dreamy looks
and thunderous smiles.
What tales she echoes,
what amazing boats
she sinks.
The breath of Europe
is recorded in the Bodensee's sighing:
the wars and agonised cries,
the shrieks of pleasure-boats,
the dying of pointless ideals.
Her castles and churches bear testimony
to all the joy and futility,
the spasms of birth,
the ruination of fine folk.

And so my good friends
let us sip the scent off our brimful lake
to forget where we're going
for at least one long breath.
Life can be good at this moment.
It will come on to rain
but the Swabian Sea
will float with stars.
The flaming blood of her heart
will break through a thousand gates.
Our songs will live
when we are gone,
and some will tremble at them
who felt like us.

Lake Constance

Flying Into Tübingen Airspace

I'm flying back
into Tübingen airspace.
I'm ready for Swabian girls of lace.
That's what makes my pulse race:
the ancient tales of flights of fancy,
the brains of grace,
the gruesome face of the rat race,
hideous screeching under my wheels.

My glowing undercarriage
simply lances
through
all the tempestuous skies
to greet my ascending loves,
the dashing ways,
and blades
of ancient grass,
with blossoming songs
skirting the hurtling runways;
bang of memory,
death of lovely moments
on the tip of my very tongue.

O Mick I miss you so,
O Julia,
O Jack the Lad.
I will recall you all ways,
your twinkling faces
as I stagger along,
in my typical afternoon drunkenness,
past all,
past all the closed bars,
the volcanic ash
of long lost poems
spat out
on dreadful floors

into the ears
of ignorant barmaids
and boring old guys
with nothing to do
but remember.

That won't happen to me.
Because I run,
across your fallen dust,
exploding,
like a proud volcano,
with the boiling lava
of brand new verse.
Run and run and run
with a fresh joy,
a new life
every day.

Tübingen Webcam

Look down from the Rathaus
and you will see me plodding
over cobbled tales.
I traipse though the clear night,
eyes stumbling across discarded dreams,
toes aching with raindrops,
my eyes sore with forgetting.
The old square undulates with the rhythm
of catcalls and pigeons
pecking at old folk's bones.
Ancient crows swoop
on market remnants,
the scent of forgotten summers
lingering in the winter's gutters.
I bowl
down the hill
lurching with words
that spill with slush
and the glitter of ice under the moon.
We are but Swabia's leaves,
blowing about in a hushed city
that baffles our loves,
scattered
on the flow of the Neckar's infernal gurgle.
We are grinning away
in our urge
for survival,
in our endurance of boredom,
the hint of romance.
Scan my breath
for more joyful moments,
pan across the skyline
to pick up the Lufthansa throb
in the beautiful clouds.
I will sing again in Tübingen .
I will kick out the glass on Melancholy Street.

I want to hear Uhland breathe in the daft breeze,
see Hölderlin brood on a raft.
This world is crazy
and my mind
rejoices in it.

Dawn Chorus, Corrensstrasse 45

Last night's red wine,
thrown to excess
down the throat
of this flowing town,
throbs in my startled veins
as a thousand blackbirds
ring in the early hours
with a cathedral of singing bells
rising though the green mist
of these fertile hills.
Careering down
Tübingen's stooped lanes,
I want to scream
wild hymns
for Johannes Kepler,
throw open
the window of my heart,
let dreams spin
completely
out of control,
making love on the morning's wing.
For I am a singer too,
sending my lyrics
across an outstretched Germany,
my wet lips seeking
those of distant lovers
waking like me
in a strange and thrilling land,
full of soaring music,
full of blackbirds
lush
with song.

Hermann Hesse in the Gutter

'We are all in the gutter, but some of us are looking at the stars.'
                                        Oscar Wilde

Headlong, headstrong
Hermann Hesse
fell, flat on his face, in the Tübingen mud.
'That's it! Get stuck into the shit!'
an ageing Swabian yelled.
And the church-bells throbbed along Lange Gasse,
and the dust fell on Heckenhauer's bookshop.
And, as young Hermann slithered to his fumbling feet
and cleaned his shitty glasses,
his first poems
shone in the moonlit gutter.

The writer Hermann Hesse (1877-1962) was born in Calw and, at the age of 19, began a four-year period of work in Heckenhauer's bookshop in Tübingen . It was then that he began writing and, during this time, he published his first poems as 'Romantic Songs'.

Hier Kotzte Goethe (Goethe Puked Here)

Goethe puked here –
he did.
Poured out a tide of words
on the street.
Couldn't stand the smell of war,
the decay of stinking empires,
ugly whiff of bad poetry.
He did –
he puked on Tübingen,
on all the drivel
coursing from the normal text books.
He had to.
To keep his guts open to the theory of beauty,
vomit out the wretched ugliness
from this town's pouting ulcers.
Clear 'Coin Alley'
for all the shouting children
to dance along,
for his mate Schiller to rhyme by,
for the swifts to sing
over it all,
over and over again
in this distinct order of loveliness.

About Goethe, the legend says that he was invited to stay in Tübingen for a while but on the very first day that he was walking around he couldn't stand the smell of the open channels and did what he had to do.

The publishing dynasty Cotta reigned over German academic life in its printed form from Tübingen's Cotta House for over 150 years. Heinrich Heine even maintained that Johann Friedrich Cotta, publisher of Schiller, Goethe, Hölderlin, Herder, Humboldt and many others, 'held his hand over all the world'. A plaque on the house recalls the legendary visit by Goethe in 1797, which is drastically commented on by another plaque on the Martinianum right next door: 'Goethe puked here'.

Carl Friedrich Kielmeyer's 1793 speech on the balance of organic forces was a turning point in Goethe's scientific development, showing that Kielmeyer, whom Goethe met in Tübingen on September 10, 1797, played a critical role in guiding his attention toward organic processes common to all species.

The Month of the Asparagus

It was the month of the asparagus
and you kissed me by the river
with the rain flowing down your face.
It was the day you burst
like a volcano,
gushing all over me
as we ran
down Neckargasse,
exulting
in the sky weeping all over us
and in the laughter of children
splashing in the damp raging day.
It was the month of the asparagus
when our dreams landed
through the attic window of Lange Gasse 18.
It was the day my heart rang
with all the bells of Tübingen
and my bones ached
with the weight of memory,
the sad loss,
hanging over us
a mountainous cloud of longing
full with the tangy moisture
of new songs and poems.
It was the month of the asparagus
when I zoomed in to meet you
with my arms open to the grand afternoon.
O what a day
when I came again to see you
with my heart heavy,
riddled with the seeds
of creative delight, and the light
of a stream of wondrous moments
pouring
the length of Wilhelmstrasse,
into the very realms of hope.

Lange Gasse 18

The leaves blow through the glass
as dreams float in the room
and people I have travelled with
climb up these timbered stairs.
Memories coat the walls,
days wander down the lane;
there is no telling where the tales
of drunken nights have gone.
Church bells punctuate the moon,
screams open up the dawn,
and I see Jennifer lying there,
poems oozing from her smiles.
At morning, Ingrid, with her little hands,
brings coffee to my brain
and Karin calls at evening's door
with wine to ease the pain.
All these dancing moments,
the dripping down of hours;
this house's chest is heaving
with the loss of human touch.
I drink those sunken days
and know the gulps are fleeting
but the moonlight-stains on the empty bed
will show we bled
for love.

City Poet

(for Ronald Ohlsen & Rense Sinkgraven, City Poets of Groningen)

I am this blue barge,
the pancake ship,
the casino of flashing neon.
I am the light in a fish's eyes,
the icy herring down the throat.

I am the City Poet.

I am the unknown lanes we stalk along,
a red shirt,
the stripper of paint.
I am death waiting at the railway station,
a Duvel in the old buffet.

I am the City Poet.

I am a museum of children,
an Irish pub out of place,
the ancient bard etching odes.
I am the word stuck in your head,
the drugs from last night.

I am the City Poet.

I am the next call,
the starlings wheeling in the dusk,
the darkness she brought you.
I am the sober priest in the drunk's tower,
the bus stop you kissed her at.

I am the City Poet.

I am a walking cinema,
the empty library,
the last one for the road.
I am the finger in her pants,
a frightening glance of yourself.

I am the City Poet.

I am this laughing church,
this gas factory,
the football game from hell.
I am a cracking goal,
the free man in a prison.

I am the City Poet.

I am a scream in a dull meeting,
the chairman of the bored,
the councillor for happiness.
I am a stinking canal,
the giggle in her blouse.

I am the City Poet.

I am a yellow train,
a flash across the countryside,
the bearer of state grants.
I am a brilliant dustman,
a spade amongst hearts.

I am the City Poet.

I am a word swimmer,
a shipbuilder who rhymes,
the planner of good times.
I am an evil messenger,
the dart in his face.

I am the City Poet.

I am these streets,
a fag in the puking gutter,
the ministry of obscure diseases.
I am your filthy town,
the tears in your homesick eyes.

I am the City Poet.

Backwater

In Hochdorf, where it always pours,
the girls are drenched
to the skin
and the birds swim
across the ocean
of the sky.
In Hochdorf
the bleeding rain
teems like history
down the drain
and the ghosts
of marching men
still sip
the blood.
In Hochdorf
a train
breaks through
the sheets of tears
in old men's eyes
and handkerchiefs wave
a stream of lives
goodbye.
In Hochdorf
the raindrops
lodge like bullets
in your brain
and all the wet children
want to sing
and drink the freedom
flooding through
their hearts.
In Hochdorf,
where it always pours.
In Hochdorf,
where it always pours.

Vismarkt

(for Rense Sinkgraven)

The Mayor is bothered
about the litter in my brain;
the dross of poems
spilled out onto bar floors
and the fishy streets of Groningen.
He prowls the gutters
of my verse,
seeking to tidy up
the rhymes
and times I slopped
erotic images
between the lines
of council meetings.
The detritus
from lost poetry readings
gathers up
in windy corners
on this market day,
curled up
into sodden memories,
dark with crumbling print.
This city's flags
continue
to flap proud,
defiant
in the rampant northern breeze,
fingers of lost empires
forlornly
waving
at laughing girls
and daring boys
dashing headlong
over stinking bones.
You will not make me clean –

I am a dirty poet
whose head aches
with dark subversive thoughts.
I am not tidy –
my very speech
remains unruly
as a mad professor in the Huis de Beurs.
I will mess up your streets
with a dynamic anarchy
until a true democracy
makes a clean breast of things
and the road-sweepers
and dreamers
of the Vismarkt
share a green and wondrous world.

Keep an Eye on the Martini Tower for Me

Keep an eye on the Martini Tower for me
while I struggle with my life.
I still miss the smell of fish
and the smoke of the Huis de Beurs.
I will be back, with another song,
for Mister Wilcox's Liberation Tour.
I will be ready for that Pancake Ship
and the drunken stools of O'Ceallaigh's.

Keep an eye on the Martini Tower for me
while I work out which view to see.
I will be shouting in a twin-town
and killing my time with romance.
I will be smashing through politicians
and drowning in red lights.
I will be rehearsing poems,
forgetting how real life hurts.

Keep an eye on the Martini Tower for me,
I'm tearing up coasts to greet you.
You'll see my ghost in Schipol,
with a pint of strong blood in a glass.
I'm on my way back to Groningen,
with the smack of three kisses on me,
to shake the warm hand of a city poet,
to piss in the face of a heckler.

Keep an eye on the Martini Tower for me,
I was happy in the Land of Cockaigne.
I could see clowns on a dismal day
and blondes in a sea of black.
I met a Grey Man with a girl of nineteen
and I asked him to show me the way.
I saw an old hand hack the guts from a beast
and sucked a cigar to be kind.

Keep an eye on the Martini Tower for me,
don't let her fly away.
I need her to hold my life together,
I crave her to show me the way.
I want her to lean my fragile bones against,
I need history to guide my feet.
I have left a careworn scarf with you,
keep it warm for when I come back.

The Lack of Music on a Den Bosch Estate

In a tide of yellow and red
I staggered with a brass band mob
at the surging Carnival.
I felt the sound of drums
and the thud of my head
as the girls lifted up their skirts
and laughed
at me.
Crammed into the Bonte Palet
with booming frogs
I supped the pouring ale of centuries;
I tore myself away from the prancing,
leapt into a cab with a cackling driver
to make it to the dimmed suburbs.
Across this field
you could barely feel
the joy and antics
of the Brabant people
in the town.
Down Palestrinastraat,
Vivaldistraat,
I groped.
Along Mozartsingel,
past Bachstraat
and Chopinstraat
to Wagnerlaan,
my heart began to ache
with the lack of music
and dancing.
On to Beethovenlaan
and Verdistraat,
to Brucknerstraat,
the curtains twitching
as I staggered,
with folk songs gone
and my tongue

emptied of lyrics.
To Schubertsingel
and, at last,
Cesar Francklaan,
the sudden silence
of a drowned village,
an orchestra shot dead
with the bullets of icy tears
from blind windows,
sullen neighbours
and their droning hymns.

Groningen Horses

Groningen horses
drag me here,
run wild in my brain,
leap in the imagery of the artist Werkman,
trot through my memories of wet streets,
jump over bars to greet me.
Their hooves clopping
through the shit of war,
they dart in the night along Guldenstraat,
wake in me dreams of the sleeping fields,
the swish of old tales
gone out of our minds.
Their withers are broad as Uncle Loek's back,
their haunches like the arse
of a woman I once knew.
What do they think of it all,
the fantasies in the Town Hall,
the pall of depression over Europe?
Stride on my sturdy Groningen beasts,
may your cannon bones,
your barrels,
your flanks,
roar with energy,
zoom across this yawning,
dawning market square
and treat these sobbing days
as if they were not there.

Swan Song

Oh you float on canals
on a head of Amstel beer.
You keep yourself white in a dirty town,
watching the tulips drown.
You skim past the red lights and the bulb-fields of traffic;
gracefully bend your vase-like neck
under a low Dutch joke.
The tall, slim houses seem to stoop
towards you;
you warn them off
with a thrust of your beak.
You feed off tourists
on floodlit transparencies
broken by rippling houseboats.
You stay drifting in memories of the Indies;
a small piece of momentary beauty,
prettier than Amsterdam,
more shapely than Holland;
a true Swan
of the World.

Sky the Guide Dog

Sky is a guide dog.
He will lick you
into light.
His eyes are pools of sparks.
He is a star hound.

Sky leads us across the universal fields,
opens up the lids of daydreams,
teaches us to feel
those tender rays.

Sky's vista runs deep,
shows up a braille galaxy.
In this cold, blind dark
we follow his moonlit trail.
We marry our lonely visions with his
and see
heaven.

Poem for a Blues Harmonica

(for Ad van Emmerik)

A poem is an organ of the mouth,
a verse I suck and blow.
It sings from my heart on the wind,
it breathes with my life.

I place my poetry between my lips
like licking my girlfriend's breasts.
I smoke it like a cigar
and squeeze the good juice from it.

My poetry is a fire,
it screams blues murders.
I craft it with my gentle fingers
and shout it around the world.

This poem is a drink wet with rhyme,
a harp in a rowdy beer museum.
I am a drunk whose rhymes stagger,
my words are music in your ear.

Chet - From a Window

(in memory of Chet Baker 1929 -1988)

The constant onslaught of Amsterdam
surged through Zeedijk
on that hot night
when a full moon
dragged you
flying to your death.
In your room,
in the Prins Hendrik Hotel,
your clothes lay
neatly folded
in your suitcase,
with your body
a foetus on the street below.
Great white hope
fallen
offstage,
a love for heroin never shaken.
Sorrow was your stuff,
a plaintive,
lyrical anguish,
an excess of gloom
and charm.

This undernourished and parched body,
a singing corpse,
searching for an uncollapsed vein,
an expert driver hating the road
and the bleak hotel of his doom.
Such a foolish love.

Oklahoma farmboy on a golden trumpet,
his teeth knocked out in San Francisco,
chained to an album a day
for a thousand dollars in cash.

And the Italian you learned in a Lucca jail,
your spirit surviving its deportation,
a lonely and melancholy master drifter
whose pianissimo
touched the soul.

Friday 13th May 1988,
Chet's heart stopped
and his horn
lost its tongue.

Love Poem

In your damp bedroom,
wet with tears, we
broke bread together,
bit
into the night
and ate,
with the crumbs
of kisses in your eyes.
Your breath
flaming like the Krakow dragon,
your teeth flashed
sharp as fire
as we
guided the slender trams into slumber
and I
promised you
fantasies
to kiss off your lights
and leave
me to nurse
my bites.

For Paul

I saw you
creeping
round Baudelaire's grave.
You were on a pilgrimage from Blyth.
I saw your face in Montparnasse,
blending with a swarm of irises.
You needed to get away from the grime,
to bathe in flowers of evil,
to wash your pale white body
in the Paris crowds,
broaden your worried brow.
Your young poems already rot
in the cemetery of poets
and yet you still churn out the stuff
as if your little voice meant something.
There is no going back
to that fateful day
when our eyes met by chance,
neighbours brought together by France
and the great mind of Charles.
He lay there
pecked at by the grip of time,
in agony,
drugged by a quickfire nib,
injected with the poison of love
and the wit of drunkenness.
I saw you
before I even met you,
and I knew that one day we would fly
to a liberated Prague together,
to taste the freedom of the streets
and the lightning lash of fate.

Grapes in Bulgaria

Grapes bulge in the searing sun,
fresh and healthy as a young girl,
rich with optimism
in a back-street vineyard.
Taste sweet as your lips, dear.
Trickle down my throat –
wine today in my poems.
Hang your head for life's sake:
the portrait, decked with black ribbons,
nailed to the door,
stares at us as we drink
blood from the glass.
Along the rails,
hurtling headlong, we
spit out the pips
from the fruit an old lady gives us;
fruit of her heart,
her old heart,
decked with black ribbons.
Black wine in the night.
Stars bunch over Bulgaria.
The rain refreshes our skin.
Peeling off our clothes,
we enter new towns,
strange rooms,
beds drenched
in yesterday's kisses.
Picture on the hotel wall
is of a grape mountain.
Climb the stairs
until your thirst is
quenched.
Sew seeds on the map.
Bulgaria, we'll squeeze you
out of love,
to live.

My Lady Dentist

She fills me
with a desperate longing;
bending over me
in her clean white tunic.
The smell of her
sets my teeth
on edge;
she drills
a sense of danger into me.
I can only salivate,
eyes popping,
as her dark hair brushes
over my face.
She stabs my gums,
makes my mouth
bleed kisses
on the National Health.
She pulls
and grinds,
and I can taste her
on my lips.
My Lady Dentist,
are all our dreams so false?
Or is it you,
in this anaesthetic haze,
wrapping your rubber gloves around me,
licking me better,
with my blood
on your tongue?

So Don't Come to My Funeral

You never knew
how beautiful I could be.
You never saw
just how blue my eyes were.
You couldn't feel me fly
and did not sense
the passion in my beating words.

So don't come to my funeral,
don't come to my funeral.

You were never there
when my heart broke.
You didn't pick me up
when my ideals drowned.
You never got drunk with me
in the sunshine of my smiles.
You never felt the love in me.

So don't come to my funeral,
don't come to my funeral.

You hemmed in my free spirit
with your overeducated mind.
You trapped the birds in my poems
and caged my strong ideas.
You couldn't act the fool
for fear you lost your face.
You never risked a dance.

So don't come to my funeral,
don't come to my funeral.

You never studied the art of chance,
the sudden surge of love in a stranger,
the golden coin in an Edinburgh gutter.

Your education controlled your heart.
Would you save me as I fell from the sky?
Would you bleed for me?
I sense not, I sense you are cold.

So don't come to my funeral,
don't come to my funeral.
I don't want to see you there.

Because you lied to me forever.
Because you couldn't play a tune in your poems.

Don't come to my funeral,
don't come to my funeral.

Leaving Friends/Friends Leaving

(in memory of Mick Standen)

I have lost my roaring boys and girls.
They are left behind,
fallen from Collegium stools;
the poignant moments in Lange Gasse dust.
Times and laughter shared
dwindled to an Ammer trickle
in a bleak semester,
worn out days.

Friends are for leaving.
I'm afraid
I am too old to chase it.
These young Swabian mistresses
are too damned quick
for me to grab anymore;
their lightning glances,
hints of a possible romance
boarding trains,
flickering
in frigid seminar rooms.

Tear yourself from me
as I stumble
through security.
I know I'll miss
your touch.

Horst has gone from Hades bar,
Paddy from the Boulanger,
Gerd has flown
to China.
Now Mick has slipped away
and all those twinning hours.

Nothing is still.
Her eyelashes flicker,
new wounds open;
the light streams on Wilhelmstrasse,
darkness fills Hafengasse.

A special sunlight
sparkles in my beer,
shafts of it
dart on the counter.
A bird flaps
across my face,
shadow
of a former glory.

So that's the story:
we lose it all,
we lose everything
and everyone.
It's why I cling
to the night wind
beating against my cheeks,
to the whisper of the leaves
along this dull suburban street.

The old voices
of mates I made
howling
through the mediocrity
of lonely petrol stations,
soul-destroying car parks.

Puddles
of former joy
winking at the moon.

We Change at Limerick Junction

We change at Limerick Junction.
Rain knocks the smiles off our faces,
the sun glows and exposes the dust
in the faint traces of our poems.
We change at Limerick Junction.
Weather makes our eyes fade,
the hours grow tired of breathing
in the pain of the world.
We change at Limerick Junction.
Hearts thunder along the crazy rails,
the weight off our feet lands
with a thump on the daily platform.
We change at Limerick Junction.
Carry gifts for old friends,
the urge to go on trailing poetry along the lines.
We change at Limerick Junction.
Girls get too young for us,
the flesh weakens with the passage of whiskey.
We change at Limerick Junction.
Air races in the manes of horses,
the money drains from our exhausted pockets.
We change at Limerick Junction.
Jump from one train to another,
the inexhaustible desire to write a better verse.
We change at Limerick Junction.
Words are why we laugh,
beauty is what makes us want to live.
We change at Limerick Junction.

About the Author

Born in Newcastle upon Tyne, where he has worked as a community development worker, poet, librarian and publisher, Keith Armstrong now resides in the seaside town of Whitley Bay. He is coordinator of the *Northern Voices* creative writing and community publishing project and has organised several community arts festivals in the region and many literary events. He was also founder of *Ostrich* poetry magazine, *Poetry North East*, *Tyneside Poets* and the *Strong Words and Durham Voices* community publishing series.

He recently compiled and edited books on the Durham Miners' Gala and on the former mining communities of County Durham, the market town of Hexham and the heritage of North Tyneside. He has been a self-employed writer since 1986 and he was awarded a doctorate in 2007 for his work on Newcastle writer Jack Common at the University of Durham where he received a BA Honours Degree in Sociology in 1995 and Masters Degree in 1998 for his studies on regional culture in the North East of England. His academic study of Jack Common was published by the University of Sunderland Press in 2009.

His poetry has been extensively published in magazines such as *New Statesman*, *Poetry Review*, *Dream Catcher*, and *Other Poetry*, as well as in the collections *The Jingling Geordie*, *Dreaming North*, *Pains of Class* and *Imagined Corners*, on cassette, LP and CD, and on radio and TV. He has performed his poetry on several occasions at the Edinburgh Fringe Festival and at literary Festivals in Aberdeen, Bradford, Cardiff, Cheltenham (twice at the Festival of Literature - with

Liz Lochhead and with 'Sounds North'), Durham, Newcastle upon Tyne, Greenwich, Lancaster, and throughout the land.

In his youth, he travelled to Paris to seek out the grave of poet Charles Baudelaire and he has been making cultural pilgrimages abroad ever since. He has toured to Russia, Georgia, Bulgaria, Poland, Iceland (including readings during the Cod War), Denmark, France, Germany (including readings at the Universities of Hamburg, Kiel, Oldenburg, Trier and Tübingen), Hungary, Italy, Ireland, Spain, Sweden, Czech Republic, The Netherlands, Cuba, Jamaica and Kenya.

Acknowledgements

These poems have been selected from the following Keith Armstrong collections and pamphlets:
Angels Playing Football: Newcastle Poems (Northern Voices)
Giving Blood (People's Publications)
Hermann Hesse in the Gutter: Tuebingen Poems (Northern Voices)
Imagined Corners (Smokestack Books)
The Jingling Geordie (The Common Trust)
Old Dog on the Isle of Woman (Cold Maverick Press Legend Series, Number 1)
Shakespeare and Company (Erdesdun Poems)

Thanks are due to the following publications where some of these poems, or versions of them, first appeared:
The Black Light Engine Room, Cherryburn Times, The Making of Saint Cuthbert (Berwick Museum Theatre Group), Other Poetry, The Recusant, Revival Literary Journal, Voices.

Some have also been anthologised in:
Bell's Caught (Tyneside Writers' Workshop)
Fishing and Folk: Life and Dialect on the North Sea Coast (Northumbria University Press)
Golden Girl: Poems on Newcastle upon Tyne (Credo Press)
Grainger Market (The Tyneside Poets)
Microphone On: Poetry from the White House Pub (White House Press, Limerick)
Paging Doctor Jazz (Shoestring Press)
Return to Cherryburn: The Life and Work of Thomas Bewick (The Tyneside Poets)

Tide Lines: A Celebration of Druridge (Druridge Bay Campaign)

Keith Armstrong's poems, including some in this selection, have been broadcast on BBC Radio Newcastle and also featured on *Sound City*: a CD with Bruce Arthur, Ian Carr, Pete Challoner, Bob Fox and Rick Taylor (Northern Voices)